THE ROLES OF ENERGY LAW

VOLUME 3, ISSUE 1 OF BRILLOPEDIA

TATHASTU PARASHAR

Contents

Preface

"Start writing, no matter what. The water does not flow until the faucet is turned on".

- Louis L'Amour

Hundreds of students and professors are contributing their work to Brillopedia, we are here to provide ample information about Law and Contemporary issues. Our aim is to provide a platform for today's generation to express their views and ideas on law and contemporary law.

Author

Publication

This research paper is published in volume 3, issue 1 of Brillopedia

CHAPTER ONE

Abstract

Develop national energy policies and regulatory frameworks that will help to create the necessary economic, social and institutional conditions in the energy sector, limited attempts by energy law scholars to ensure that their research impacts upon legal practice and in particular upon the decision-making of judges. One of the aims of this article is to address this issue and call for the need of energy law scholars to re-engage with what their sub-discipline of law is and also to provide new scholarship that can bridge the gap between academics and professionals in energy law. This article aims to begin a wider movement across the energy law field of scholars with the aim of initiating and advancing the aim and direction of energy law.environmental impact assessment is now widely used by many nations to determine what sort of new energy systems should be licensed. In addition to air pollution issues, environmental impact assessments feature in environmental laws and are now a mature legal system established in all regions.

Introduction

The spotlights on energy regulation's commitment to the energy change and to explore on that progress. It is notable that regulation assumes an essential part in overseeing the energy area and has central ramifications for the quest for the low-carbon progress. Regardless of this reality, regulation frequently stays kept to its storehouse, blocked off to non-legal counselors because of its particular systemic qualities and inner language. means to start an open discourse between energy regulation and other energy-centered disciplines. It initially makes sense of how energy regulation, as a legitimate discipline, ought to be figured out in this unique situation and what that suggests for energy regulation as an arrangement of administration. It then investigates the connection point between energy regulation and different disciplines in which examination into the energy progress is completed. The recognizes and assesses the jobs of energy regulation in the energy change, finishing up with a rundown of the ramifications of the job of energy regulation for the energy progress and for energy research.

CHAPTER THREE

The relationship between energy law and research

The energy change requires significant commitments from state run administrations and administration, people, the confidential area and the scholastic local area leading exploration on the energy progress. The spotlights on the commitment of energy regulation to the energy change and to the insightful investigation of that progress.despite the fact that law has undeniable consequences on the energy transition, there is a dearth of knowledge of the functions of law in this body of study and in the energy transition. This article fills in this knowledge vacuum by examining how energy law has affected the energy shift and what that means for future energy research. The article's foundation is a qualitative examination of the body of work at the nexus of energy law studies, jurisprudence, and energy research. energy law study has emphasised the importance of concepts like national resource sovereignty, energy justice, and halting climate change. Scholars who investigate energy laws from the viewpoints of other disciplines are also likely to be aware of and have access to the key features of energy law.

provides trustworthy information about the causes of the energy transition's need and the methods for achieving it (Hansen and others, 2016). Scientific methods also show issues with the energy transition that need to be resolved, whether they are of a social, economic, technological, or physical origin. The goal of research is also to solve these issues.

The energy business has always been driven by technological advancement brought about by research, but the energy transition is where the significance of technological innovation is most clearly shown. The fact that research "has long functioned as both a driver and an informant in regard to the sustainable energy transition" has been effectively underlined.

energy transition, energy research can inform and motivate the required policy actions and ensuing lawmaking, for instance by establishing moral frameworks.

CHAPTER FOUR

Energy law's functions in the energy transition

In fact, policy and lawmaking should carefully consider the knowledge arising from scientific processes in order to assist the technical progress and innovation required in the energy transition. Along with driving and supplying information into the legislative process, energy research also plays a crucial role in the interpretation of already-existing legislation. When energy research results in recommendations for how the law should be interpreted or evolved in fields like social science or engineering, it can also provide important insights for energy law as a legal discipline.Energy law's role can be restrictive, in which case it establishes limits, restrictions, or even explicit bans in regard to the changes required for the energy transition. In its most basic form, a restriction might come from a piece of legislation that acts as a deterrent to actions that would otherwise be advantageous for the energy transition. For instance, zoning regulations or environmental permit procedures may hinder, postpone, or even impede the implementation of renewable energy projects.the role of energy law may become constrictive for a number of reasons. While the emergence of a restricted function is more likely to be accidental, the legislator is likely to have intended for energy law to act as a facilitator of the energy transition. In this situation, the lawmaker may have passed a bill without considering how it will affect the energy sector and for a reason unrelated to the energy sector particularly. Energy laws can also operate independently of one another. There are many instances where the legal frameworks for various energy carriers and infrastructures do not converge, despite the fact that these frameworks are normally different.Legal solutions may have limiting consequences because they have not yet been updated to reflect the needs of the technological or economic advances taking place in the actual world. The legislative process is frequently slower than the energy transition itself. For instance, given that unbundling standards have been extensively accepted and call for the separation of supply and generating activities from network operation, some countries have had difficulty classifying energy storage.Pursuing the energy transition involves legal instruments on many fronts, answering a myriad of concerns, as it represents a fundamental transformation in how energy is produced and consumed. Even if institutions concentrate on law-making just within their areas of expertise without cross-sectoral cooperation between the energy industry and other sectors, a well-functioning legal solution to one problem can have restrictive, undesirable implications in respect to another. Energy law may play a guiding role in the energy transition, acting as a navigator to direct developments that occur or need to occur during the shift. For instance, the government may decide that renewable energy projects are eligible for subsidisation while fossil fuel projects are not, giving low-carbon energy operations an economic advantage and directing investment toward low-carbon goals.

Energy law is likely to be supportive of an energy efficiency software company, but it's also possible that sectors like data privacy law will impose legal constraints. The essential institutional and human rights framework is established by constitutional legislation. It frequently upholds values like the rule of law and, more crucially from the perspective of encouraging investments in low-carbon energy, legal clarity, regulatory predictability, and legitimate expectations. These legal foundations are crucial for luring in the huge quantities of investment required for the energy transition.

CHAPTER FIVE

Conclusion

By describing what energy law is, how it connects to and interacts with energy research, and how it can facilitate, restrict, and guide the energy transition, the contribution of energy law to the energy transition and to research into it is made. This investigation has important ramifications for how energy research, energy law, and the energy transition interact. In order to enlighten energy law on the challenges that legislators should address in the energy transition and to feed into the research questions and legal interpretations made in energy law scholarship, energy research in fields other than law has a crucial role to play. To put it another way, energy research can assist in providing the information and instruments to correct flaws or weaknesses in energy law and to provide input for energy.